ACCELERATE YOUR PATH TO FINANCIAL FREEDOM

Stop Making These 10 Biggest Financial Mistakes!

GERAINT LIU

ISBN
978-1-5437-4727-0 (sc)
978-1-5437-4728-7 (e)

Library of Congress Control Number: 2018955180

Print information available on the last page.

To order additional copies of this book, contact
Toll Free 800 101 2657 (Singapore)
Toll Free 1 800 81 7340 (Malaysia)
www.partridgepublishing.com/singapore
orders.singapore@partridgepublishing.com

08/17/2018

PARTRIDGE

Table Of Contents

Introduction

Congratulations on taking the first step towards achieving financial freedom! You could have invested your time on lots of other things but you have decided to invest it in your financial future.

"Financial Freedom" has different meanings to different people. Whatever your definition of financial freedom may be, I'm sure we both can agree that it'll be great if we do not have to constantly worry about money.

There's a saying that goes, **"It takes a wise man to learn from his mistakes, but an even wiser man to learn from others."**

As a Financial Strategist, I have witnessed many people either suffering or missing their goals due to making poor financial decisions and it always came down to 2 main causes.

It was always either due to:

• the lack of knowledge; or
• the lack of action.

Thus, my aim with this guide is to bring you closer to your definition of financial freedom by raising your awareness on the **10 biggest financial mistakes** that you might be making and at the same time empower yourself with the knowledge on how you can avoid them.

Introduction

If you are reading this book, chances are you are not 100% satisfied with where you are now in your financial life.

You want to make changes too and move yourself towards achieving financial freedom. This thought could come from any of the following reasons:

1. You want to be **more self-reliant financially,** be less dependent on others and have more control over your finances.

2. You want to **generate multiple streams of income** so you don't have to rely solely on your day job.

3. You want to have **more freedom**. You are tired of being a slave to the rat race and the corporate ladder; sacrificing precious time from your loved ones and you want to live the lifestyle you desire.

These are all great reasons to redesign your financial destiny.

In the pages that follow, I'll show you how.

Introduction

There are many who are driven and hardworking, but they don't have a clear idea of what they want in life, thus they are unable to achieve the results they deserve.

It pains me to see families suffering financially just because they don't have the knowledge to make the necessary changes.

Thus, I've adopted the best strategies from some of the region's top wealth coaches, and I'm intending to impart both these skills and knowledge that I've learnt to you so that you will be empowered to take action and make changes to your financial life.

So, if you want to have absolute clarity as to what you want to achieve, and the exact steps you need to reach financial freedom, keep reading.

How To Use This Guide

Some of the tips contained in this book might apply to your particular situation while some might not. The key is taking the bits that's relevant to you and implementing them.

I have organized the mistakes in order, starting from the most important first.

On the next page I developed a **Financial Success Map** for you which is also a graphical explanation on what I'll be sharing with you on in this book.

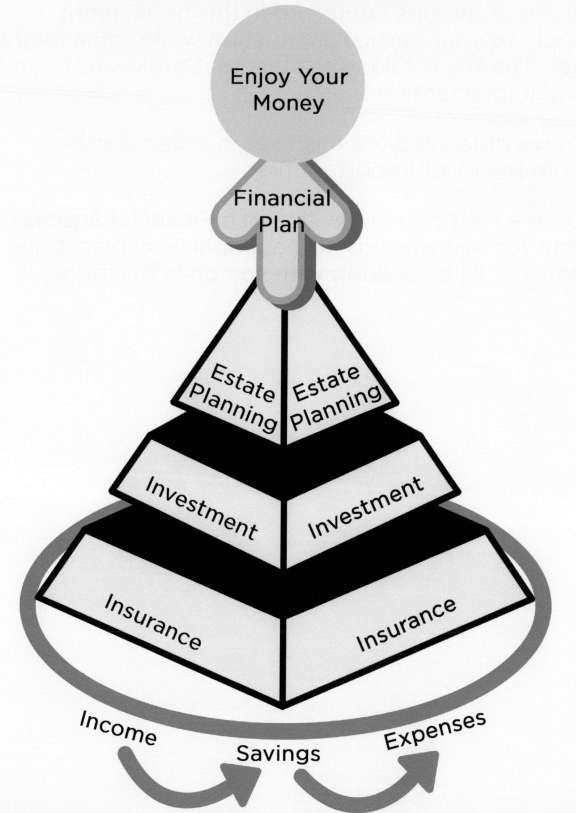

To get the most out of this guide, I suggest you take the following steps:

1. Read one section at a time

2. Highlight and take notes as necessary

3. Take one piece of information from each section you read and put it into action immediately. If you can't put it into action immediately, make a note to put it into practice as soon as possible.

Please do not just read this guide and forget about it. If you do this, you'll miss out on the guide's full potential!

Again, congratulations on investing in yourself. Just make sure you put your investment to good use!

Geraint Liu

Mistake 1: Having a Poverty Mindset

"I work so hard and I still can't get a pay raise!"

"It's my employer's fault for not paying me enough."

"I'm just not good enough for that promotion."

Do any of these sound familiar to you?

A poverty mindset arises when you let your mind wander and feed on negative self-talk!

Here are 3 signs that indicate that you have a poverty mindset:

1. Blame:

You blame everything and everyone but yourself.

Part of having the poverty mindset is having a victim mentality.

You feel that you are a powerless victim of external circumstances and you have no control over your life.

You say things like:

"My parents sent me to a lousy school that's why I can't find a good job."

"I'm not making enough because my employer doesn't like me."

When you blame others, you acknowledge to your subconscious mind that you don't have control over your decisions and the outcomes of your life, let alone your own finances.

2. Justify:

You justify your situation by telling yourself you don't really care.

You say things like:

"Actually, money doesn't really matter that much to me."

Maybe having money really isn't all that important to you, and if you are contented with where you are now then you are perfectly fine.

The danger lies after you consoled yourself and start resting on your laurels. You become lazy, stop seeking any form of self-development and neglect making any long term financial goals.

3. Complain:

You complain about your situation.

When you complain, you are focusing on the negativity in your life and the more you focus on the negativity, the more negative events will seem to happen to you.

You say things like:

"My boss just gave me more work to do and I'm not even getting a higher pay!"

You will be so focused on the risks that you will miss out on the possibilities in opportunities that could positively change your life.

Take the above scenario for example.

If you could shift your mentality, you are actually given an opportunity to prove to your boss that you are capable of handling extra work and he may shortlist you for a promotion!

I understand that sometimes it's hard to control your thoughts and how you react to them, I occasionally blame, justify and complain without realizing it too.

That is why I narrowed down these 3 tips to help the both of us out.

Tips:

If you have identified and acknowledged that you have a poverty mindset, congratulations on taking the first step.

The next step is to develop a prosperity mindset. So how are you supposed to do that?

Here are 3 tips to help you out.

1. Take Responsibility

"I am the Master of my Fate and the Captain of my Soul" – Willian Ernest Henley.

Accept that whatever situation you are in now is the result of your own decisions. Most importantly, recognize that you have the power to control your own life.

2. Surround Yourself with Positive People

"You are the average of 5 people you surround yourself with."- Jim Rohn

Watch who you are spending most of your time with. If you are constantly surrounded by friends who are negative, you can expect yourself to have a negative mindset too.

Remember, your thoughts control your emotions which control your actions.

3. Take Massive Action

Take massive action to improve yourself.

Part of having a prosperity mindset is the obsession for self-development.

Sign up for online courses, seminars, workshops to improve your skills and enhance your knowledge! Go for networking events to develop your social skills and make new friends!

Surround yourself with positive people and divert your attention towards developing yourself then there will be no room for any negativity to exist!

Mistake 2: Not Earning Enough

"Huh? What?! How is not earning enough money my mistake? I don't even have control over my salary!"

Again, if you blame, justify or complain, it's a sign that you may have a poverty mindset.

Don't forget, you have power and control over your life!

Here are 3 reasons why you might not be earning enough.

1. You are not willing to go the extra mile

"You can't have a million dollar dream with a minimum wage ethic" – Stephen C Hogan

If you're a salaried worker and you only do the minimum work that's required, it wouldn't be fair to the rest if you got the pay raise.

I understand that it can be tough to go above and beyond your job scope as you know that you may not be rewarded for the additional tasks you do, but if you can cultivate the mindset of doing more than you're paid for, you'll eventually be paid for more than you do.

Tip:

If you are a salaried worker, volunteer to take on extra workload and help your colleagues and bosses out. Prove to your superiors and yourself that you can take on additional responsibilities. Show that you are capable of handling stress.

If you run a business, bring more value to your customers. Listen to their problems and develop solutions to solve them. Show them you care and appreciate their business.

Remember, **if you are willing to do more than you are paid to do, eventually you will be paid to do more than you do.**

2. You assume

Wait! Before working your butt off, the last thing you want is to do is to spend 3 years taking on other people's workload when the criteria for a promotion is getting a Master's degree.

Tip:

Let your boss know that you're interested in the pay raise/promotion and you wish to clarify with him on what the criteria is for getting it.

Once you're confident that you've met all the criteria and you're still not getting what you're looking for, all you need to do is just ask your boss for the raise/promotion politely.

"Ask and it will be given to you, seek and you shall find, knock and the door will be opened to you" – Matthew

3. Turning Down Extra Income Opportunities

Did you know that the average millionaire has 7 streams of income? If you only rely on your job for income, you are putting yourself at great financial risk.

Are you aware that when you don't receive any pay increment and bonuses, you are losing money due to inflation?

What's inflation? Inflation is basically the rise in prices of goods and services and if your income doesn't grow faster than inflation, your income shrinks by the day.

Take for example a plate of chicken rice. How much did it cost 10 years ago? how much does it cost now? Now that's inflation!

But what's even worse than having diminishing income is not having any income at all! Imagine your company suddenly decides to lay you off, what are you going to live on then?

Tips:

Thankfully, there are tons of ways to make extra money. Here are 3 practical ways that you can start immediately.

1. Sell Your Clutter

Sell your whatever that you do not need. You can sell your stuff online through platforms like eBay and Carousell or in person through flea markets and pawnshops!

2. Tutor Someone

I believe we are all great at something, or at least good enough to be a teacher. Are you good in Math? Languages? Playing the Guitar? Get paid to teach someone!

3. Invest Your Money

There are 2 ways you can go about investing your money. You can either invest yourself or pay someone to do it.

If you prefer to invest yourself, it is recommended to spend some time to study that topic and develop your knowledge and skills in that area.

If you prefer a hassle-free way then it'll be wise to hire a professional to invest for you, you can consider investing in index funds or mutual funds through intermediaries like banks, insurance companies and various online platforms.

Mistake 3: Excessive Spending

Overspending has been the main cause of most financial problems and it has to do with one's individual lifestyle choices.

The biggest reason why people spend excessively is because they want to maintain a certain image or a lifestyle.

Most people just don't want to be looked down upon and feel inferior. They also prefer instant gratification over planning for long term financial goals.

Some examples of overspending include:

• draining your bank account on travel holidays,

• taking on excessive credit card debt for shopping; and

• over-committing to a new house or car.

Put simply, living beyond your means!

The lack of control on your spending usually results in:

• taking on additional debt

• not being able to save for financial goals

• not being able to afford insurance to protect your wealth

• not having enough to invest to grow your wealth

Tips:

If you are serious about achieving financial freedom, it is important to keep your spending under control. Here are 2 tips for you.

1. Budgeting

If you're new to budgeting, this 50-20-30 rule is a great starting point to help you out.

• **50%** of your income should go to **living expenses**

o Eg. Phone Bills, Utilities, Loans, Insurance, Groceries, Transport

• **20%** of your income should go to your **financial goals**

o Eg. Wedding, Home purchase, Retirement, Investment

• **30%** of your income should go to **flexible spending**

o Eg. Movies, Travel

So that's 80% spending and 20% savings/ investment.

Feel free to be flexible with this rule, but you have to **at least set aside 20% for your financial goals.**

2. Track Your Expenses

Setting up a budget is a great first step, but if you don't track your expenses, it's extremely hard to stick to your budget!

So how do you track your expenses?

Use a money tracking mobile app of course! It's incredibly tedious in the beginning, but it'll do you good in the future.

It's important to track every single cent that you spent. This is so that you'll know exactly where your money disappears to and you'll think twice about impulse spending again!

Mistake 4: Taking on Too Much Debt

With regards to credit cards and personal loans, many people take on debt because they cannot keep their spending under control.

As we have seen earlier, overspending can be a source for major financial problems and one of the causes is taking on too much debt.

Here are 3 signs to know if you have too much debt.

1. You have difficulty paying your bills on time

You pay your bills late because you don't have enough savings is a huge warning sign!

Paying your bills late only snowballs your debt problems because you now have to deal with both **late payment charges** and **higher interest charges.**

2. You lose sleep worrying about your debts

When you start getting worried about not being able to repay your debt and your health suffers, it'll affect the other aspects of your life too.

3. Your credit score suffers

A credit score is a number that indicates to lenders the probability of you repaying your debts.

The score is dependent on several factors such as your credit history. The more often you repay your debt late, the lower your score gets.

Having a low credit score will have adverse effects on your borrowing in the future such as getting a housing loan.

Tips:

Stick to your Budget

I cannot stress this enough, if you manage to control your expenses, you'll know how much you're spending and you won't have any problems with debt. Prevention is always better than cure.

However, if you are already deep in debt, and want to get out of it, here are 2 repayment strategies to help you out.

1. Pay off the highest interest debt first

First, pay the minimum payment on every single debt you have so you don't incur charges, then pay off the debt with the highest interest rate first, working your way down to the debt with the lowest interest rate.

2. Repay your debt with another debt of a lower interest rate.

First, identify how high the interest rate on your current debt is. Next, take on another debt that has a lower interest rate to repay your current debt which has a higher interest rate and work your way down to the debt with the lowest interest rate.

Mistake 5: Not Saving Enough

Not saving enough is extremely dangerous, because if you do not have enough money to tide you through bad times such as a retrenchment, you will literally be eating grass!

There are 2 reasons why you are not saving enough.

1. Overspending

Overspending is the root cause of all your financial problems.

Controlling your spending is extremely important if you want to enhance your standard of living. As contradicting as it sounds, living beyond your means has a domino effect, you'll understand why later!

2. You Pay Your Bills First

A common mistake many people make is that they pay their bills and other expenses first before saving the rest.

This commonly results in having minimal savings or no savings at all at the end of the month!

Tips: Here are 3 tips to get you started.

1. Set Up an Emergency Funds

As a general good rule of thumb, you should save at least 3 to 6 months' worth of living expenses.

This will get you through in case of any emergencies.

2. Reduce Your Expenses

Once you've tracked your expenses and have found out what is causing your bank account to deplete, identify the biggest living expense and find ways to reduce it.

• Is it your phone bills? Change to a different provider.

• Is it your insurance? Ask your Financial Advisor to conduct a policy review for you and check if you are overpaying for any duplicated coverage.

3. Pay Yourself First

Automate your savings so you save first before spending the rest using 1 of these 2 ways.

3a) Talk to your HR

Tell the HR of your company to transfer your salary to another bank account. Next, you can manually transfer or set up an automatic transfer to transfer what you wish you spend from your savings account to your spending account.

3b) Save in a Savings Plan

Alternatively, you can get yourself a savings plan from an insurance company, which automatically transfers your money from your savings account into the savings plan.

The point is, as long as you don't see it, you won't be tempted to spend it

Mistake 6: Not Having The Right Insurance

Insurance is the fundamental block of any financial portfolio as it help you to transfer the risk of financial loss to an external party.

It is crucial to have insurance for your car, your house and your own life.

Unfortunately, many people have bought insurance that are simply unsuitable for their needs.

This could be due to numerous reasons such as

• unscrupulous agents prioritising their interest over consumers,

• miscommunication between the agent and consumer or

• consumer's lack of knowledge when he decides to purchase by himself

This results in you either being over-insured or under-insured and both can have adverse effects on your financial future.

Under-Insured

We all know that if you are under-insured, you are putting yourself and your loved ones at great risk.

For example, if you didn't get covered for hospital bills and you contract cancer, you won't have enough to afford the medical treatment.

A relative of mine had a heart attack which resulted in him behind in a coma. After 2 years, his family could not afford the hefty medical bills and he had to be transferred to a hospice care where he passed on a year later. For the 3 years, the whole family struggled emotionally and financially just to make ends meet.

He could have prevented his family from suffering financially if only he had comprehensive coverage.

Over-Insured

If you are over-insured, it usually means 2 things. You are holding on to policies with overlapping coverage or you are paying much more than what you can afford.

• If you have overlapping coverage you are throwing good money away because you are not allowed to profit from a claim.

• If you are paying more than you can afford, you are losing out on interest that could have been earned if you have invested the money.

Tips:

So how do you find out if you are under-insured or over-insured? Here are 2 tips.

1. Do Your Homework

Research on what are the kinds of plans you need in your current phase of life. There are even online comparison websites for you to compare different policies.

However, if you are going to compare products online, I would like to give you a heads up that financial products are all designed slightly different from each other even if they are the "same class". Comparison sites make it seem like an apple to apple comparison but in reality it isn't.

For example, if you compare 2 Life Insurance Policies online, they'll show you the differences in the sum assured and price but not every benefit and information is revealed there.

So you could be looking at a life insurance policy that is slightly more expensive but has many other benefits which are not revealed on the comparison sites.

So how much should you set aside for insurance?

Approximately **10-15% of your income** on insurance will do to make sure you don't overspend on them.

If you prefer to work with a Financial Advisor, do some research on him.

Designations such as **Certified Financial Planner (CFP)** and **Chartered Financial Consultant (ChFC)** show that he is committed to the business and he upholds a certain standard of competence and ethics.

2. Consult a Trustworthy Financial Advisor

These designations are great indicators, but that alone is not enough to determine a Financial Advisor's character.

A great way to determine if your Financial Advisor places your interests over his is that he will take the time to understand your current situation and identify your needs first before recommending any financial products.

Mistake 7: Not Investing Earlier

"Compound interest is the 8th wonder of the world. He who understands it, earns it, he who doesn't pays it." – Albert Einstein

A common mistake is waiting to invest, you are losing money every year through inflation when you let your money sit in the bank.

Not to mention, you are not losing out on extra money from the interest you could have earned!

I have identified 3 reasons why most people do not invest.

1. Not Enough Money

Remember the snowball effect? If you overspend, you won't have much to save let alone invest! If you always prioritise instant gratification over your long-term goals, you will never find the money to start investing.

2. Not Investing in Yourself First

Not investing in your own personal development first before investing yourself is dangerous. You have a high chance of losing a lot of money if you just jump in. It's like expecting to be able to swim without taking any swimming lessons.

Also, if you don't enhance your knowledge and skills about the investing world, of course you would be afraid of taking risks. Furthermore, without sufficient knowledge, you'll be more susceptible to becoming a victim of an investment scam too!

3. Not Enough Time

This is a common one. I agree that learning how to invest and then investing yourself such as analysing stocks and trading foreign currencies can be really time consuming. That is why index funds and mutual funds are invented.

Just leave it to these professionals to handle it for you.

Tips:

1. Stick To Your Budget

Control your spending, save up money then you'll have enough to invest. Investing isn't expensive, not investing is

2. Educate Yourself

There are tons of information in the internet. Attend seminars, workshops, practice with a paper money (online money) account.

Remember, if you want to develop a prosperity mindset, invest time and money to develop yourself.

3. Invest with a Professional

Like I said, invest in index funds and/or mutual funds. Fund managers and their team of analysts are there to manage the funds for you. Intemediaries like banks, brokers and insurance companies provide analytical services that help you to track these funds too.

Investment is the only way to have your money to work for you, instead of you having to work for money.

What is Estate Planning?

Estate planning is about creating a plan to distribute your estate by providing instructions stating:

• who you want to receive,

• what you want them to receive; and

• when you want them to receive the things that you own after your death.

Your estate comprises of everything you own, such as your home, insurance, savings, car.

You can do so by writing a will or a trust.

Here are 5 main differences between a will and a trust:

1. A will takes effect after you pass away, while a trust takes effect as soon as you create it.

2. With a will, you can only distribute your assets after your death, while if you have a trust, you can distribute them any time before or after death.

3. A will requires a court to oversee the execution process, thus you'll need to appoint a lawyer.
A trust on the other hand does not require supervision from the court.

4. With a will, you can give additional instructions like the upbringing of your children, while a trust is only for the distribution purposes.

5. A will becomes a public record while a trust can remain private.

Here are 2 reasons why you need estate planning.

1. You have no control over your estate

Without a will, your estate will be distributed by Singapore's intestacy rules which you have no control over and the result may not be what you wanted.

2. You can help your loved ones save time & money

Failing to plan for your estate can be time consuming and expensive for your loved ones.

After you pass on, they have to appoint lawyers, accountants and tax specialists to settle the distribution process which is costly and troublesome.

It also reduces the total available amount for distribution to your loved ones.

Tips:

Seek help from Lawyers and Financial Advisors who specialize in the area of estate planning. A Financial Advisor who has an Associate Estate Planning Practitioner (AEPP) designation has more specialized knowledge in the area of estate planning.

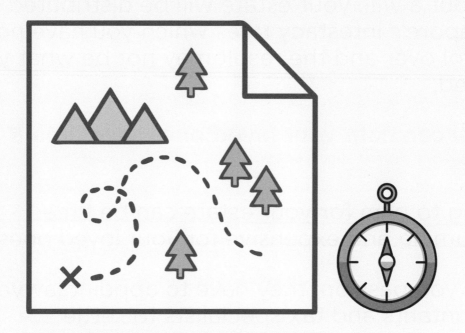

By now, you would have understood the importance of Cashflow Management (Income, Savings, Spending, Debt) and the 3 main building blocks of a financial portfolio (Insurance, Investment, Estate Planning).

To tie everything together, you will need a financial plan.

Here are 3 reasons why you need a financial plan

1. It gives you clarity

Having a financial plan is like having a compass, a map and a watch in a jungle. It identifies the destination and direction you are heading in and shows you how and when you'll arrive at your destination. If you don't have a plan, you could get lost and be unprepared to face the unexpected.

2. It improves your standard of living

A financial plan can improve your standard of living by:

• Adding another stream of income through the right investments

• Accumulating your savings so you have more to spend on your dream wedding.

• Preventing you from getting derailed from your financial goals with the right insurance.

The benefits are endless. Ultimately, it'll improve your standard of living if you act on a solid plan.

3. You can spend guilt free

Most importantly, if you have allocated your finances properly every month, you'd be able to spend guilt-free which I'll talk about later.

So how do you create a financial plan? Here are 2 ways you can go about doing it.

Tip:

1. Do It Yourself

Here is a brief 4 step guide on how to plan for yourself.

Step 1: Set Goals

Establish your long term and short term goals and make sure they are SMART goals.

Specific, Measurable, Actions-Oriented, Realistic and Time-Bound

Ask yourself questions like:

- What do I want to achieve?
- What kind of lifestyle do you want to live?
- What's your investment risk appetite like?
- When do you want to achieve it?
- How do you want to achieve it?

Step 2: Analyze Your Current Situation

Ask yourself questions like:

- How much savings do I have now?
- How much am I making now?
- Will my income and expenses increase in the near future?

Step 3: Strategize a Plan

Ask yourself questions like:

- What do I need to do to achieve my goals?

- How much do I invest or save?

- Where do I invest and save?

- When do I need to take out my money?

Step 4: Execute Your Plan

Remember my tip for the first mistake about taking massive action? If you want to change, take massive action to execute your plan.

If there are any hiccups along the way, find ways to work around it or consult a Financial Advisor.

Although I'ld like to give you a heads up that some financial mistakes are just too great even for the best Financial Advisors to correct. This leads me to option 2.

2. Consult a Financial Advisor

This is a simpler and safer option.

A competent and trustworthy Financial Advisor will be able to help you identify your goals and develop a plan that will take you a step closer towards the lifestyle you desire.

If you have any hiccups along the way, he'll just be a phone call away to help you prevent your financial problems from accumulating into a giant snowball.

Mistake 10: Not Enjoying Your Money

Finally, the most common mistake of all, not fully enjoying your money.

As I've mentioned, one of the main reasons why you need a financial plan is so that you can spend guilt-free and enjoy the fruits of your labour.

Even if you are the most frivolous and impulsive spender in the world, and you're enjoying your money now, a part of you knows that you'll have to pay the price in the future. And you'll start to feel guilty and regretful sooner or later.

Won't you agree with me that it's quite sad that you're unable to fully enjoy your own money that you have worked so hard for?

Don't you wish you could:

• travel around the world,

• enjoy your dream wedding,

• live in the house you always wanted,

• enjoy a comfortable retirement without worrying about outspending or outliving your savings; and

• spend on whatever you like knowing you are still on track towards your financial goals?

Tip:

Well, it's not a fairy tale if you:

• Managed to have your emergency fund in place,

• Significantly increased your income

• Allocated the right amount of money towards your insurance, savings and investments each month that brings you closer to both your short term and long term goals

You can be assured that you would be able to spend the rest of your money absolutely guilt free.

Conclusion

Now that I've given you:

• A heads up on the 10 biggest money mistakes commonly made that's preventing you from achieving your financial goals,

• Numerous actionable tips on how you can prevent and correct your mistakes,

• A step-by-step guide on how to achieve the financial goals that you desire,

I hope this knowledge will bring you a step closer towards Financial Freedom.

I'd also like to gently remind you with this quote, **"Nothing will change unless you change."**

Take massive action today!

How?

I understand that you may not know how to start taking action with your newly acquired knowledge.

I also know that the information I've given you is very brief, as this guide is meant to give you ideas that you can further research on by yourself.

So I just want to let you know that you have 2 choices.

You can either go through this journey alone or you can have a friend to guide you along each step of the way to reach your financial goals and solve your problems along the way.

If you do decide to work on your financial goals with me, I would be more than happy to share with you some of my financial tips and strategies that my team and I have developed.

If you decide to venture on this journey alone or with someone else, I'll continue to share with you more useful financial tips on my website and social media platforms. In any case, I wish you all the best in achieving Financial Freedom.

Your Friend,
Geraint Liu

About The Author

Geraint is a Financial Strategist with one of the leading Financial Institutions in the world, specializing in helping families achieve financial freedom.

Geraint is also the Creator of "The Financial Freedom Program (TFFP)", a 60 minutes consultation to help families achieve financial freedom and the Founder of "FirstHomeFinance. sg", a Financial Education Website for future and current home owners.

After witnessing many of his loved ones suffer from poor financial advice, he is dedicated to pursue his vision and mission of creating a financially educated, empowered and enlightened society, where everyone helps each other out by paying forward what they have learnt.

If you'ld like to learn more about Geraint, you can visit his website at www.geraintliu.com and connect with him on Facebook, Instagram and Linkedin too.

Printed in the United States
By Bookmasters